MYSTIC PERFECTIONS

MATERIALISTIC PERFECTIONS

RAMANANDA CAITANYA CANDRA DAS

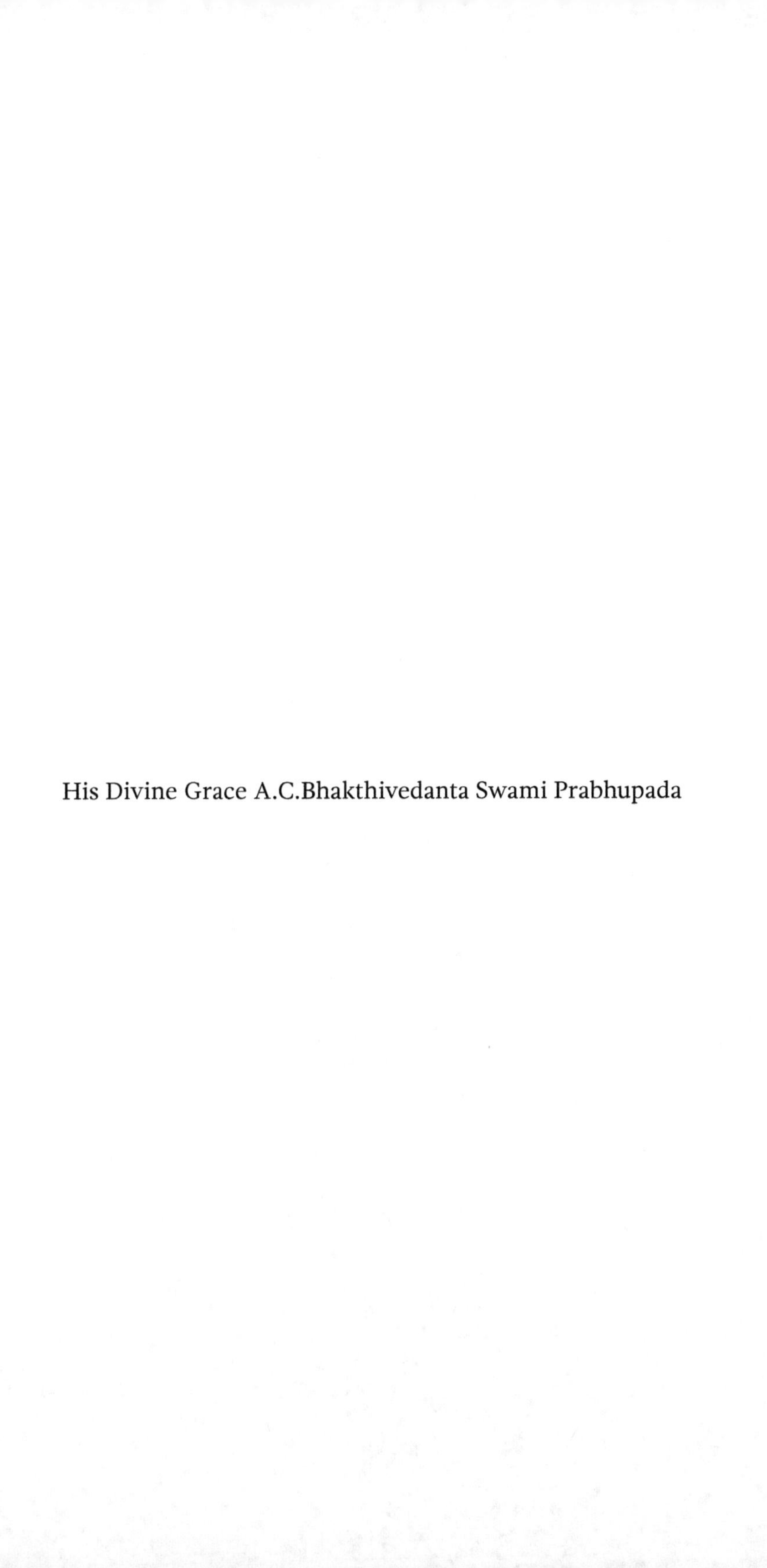

His Divine Grace A.C.Bhakthivedanta Swami Prabhupada

Contents

Acknowledgements — vii

1. Definition Of Mysticism — 1

2. Mystic Perfections — 5

3. How To Achieve Mystic Perfection — 10

4. Divine And Demoniac Mystic Powers — 18

Acknowledgements

Bhakthivedanta Book Trust

CHAPTER ONE

DEFINITION OF MYSTICISM

Definition of Mysticism

Yogeśvara: She asks for a definition of the word "occult." What is something that is occult, something occult, or mystic? What is it?

Prabhupāda: Mystic?

Yogeśvara: Mystic. What is mysticism?

Prabhupāda: I do not say anything on mysticism. Mystic, something, it is called rahasya.

Yogeśvara: Rahasya?

Prabhupāda: Rahasya. Something wonderful. Is that meaning, mystic?

Indian man: Mystic... I mean. I think when Western historians and literators explain Indian religious literature, especially literature of bhakti-mārga, they term that those are the mystics, and also they term the Sufi poets are mystics.

Prabhupāda: ...say mystic means rahasya.

Yogeśvara: Rahasya.

Prabhupāda: Rahasya means it is little difficult to understand.

Prabhupāda: Just like Kṛṣṇa says in the Bhagavad-gītā, rahasyam, rahasyam etad uttamam. Rahasyam etad uttamam. This Bhagavad-gītā is the first-class mystic. Rahasyam etad uttamaṁ, bhakto 'si me priyo 'si me [Bg. 4.3] = "Because you are My devotee, you are My dear friend, you'll understand."

So mysticism is not understandable by common man. It requires a special qualification. Just like to understand, it is also mysticism---understand, to understand God. This is also mystic. It is not understandable by ordinary man.

Room Conversation with French Nun, Type: Conversation, Date: Aug. 13, 1973, Location: Paris

Mystic power

So the devotee, he doesn't require to acquire any mystic power. What mystic power Prahlāda could attain? He was only five years old. So there was no opportunity of acquiring any mystic power. But he was being protected by the supreme mystic, Kṛṣṇa. That should be a devotee's point of view. Don't waste your time for acquiring so-called mystic power. Just devote yourself to remain a pure devotee of Kṛṣṇa, and you become the supreme mystic. That is confirmed in the Bhagavad-gītā:

yoginām api sarveṣāṁ

mad-gatenāntarātmanā

śraddhāvān bhajate yo māṁ

sa me yuktatamo mataḥ

[Bg. 6.47]

There are many yogīs, mystics, but Kṛṣṇa confirms that "Of all the yogīs, of all the mystic, a person who is always thinking of Me," śraddhāvān bhajate yo mām, yoginām api sarveṣāṁ mad-gatenāntarātmanā, "always thinking Me, Kṛṣṇa, within himself:

Hare Kṛṣṇa, Hare Kṛṣṇa, Kṛṣṇa Kṛṣṇa, Hare Hare

Hare Rāma, Hare Rāma, Rāma Rāma, Hare Hare."

So Kṛṣṇa said, "he is the best yogī." Yoginām api sarveṣāṁ. Sarveṣam means "of all." "Of all kinds of yogīs, the best yogī is who is always thinking of Me."

Lectures and Addresses,Date: May 25, 1975, Location: Honolulu

Lord Ṛṣabhadeva neglected all the mystic powers

Lord Ṛṣabhadeva neglected all the mystic powers for which the so-called yogīs hanker. Because of the beauty of devotional service, devotees are not at all interested in so-called mystic power. The master of all yogic power, Lord Kṛṣṇa, can exhibit all powers on behalf of His devotee. Devotional service is more valuable than yogic mystic powers. Devotees who are sometimes misled aspire for liberation and mystic powers. The Supreme Lord gives these devotees whatever they desire, but they cannot attain the most important function of devotional service. Devotional service to the Lord is guaranteed for those who do not desire liberation and mystic power.

S.B.5.1.6. Introduction

Yasyājñayā bhramati sambhṛta-kāla-cakro. Kāla-cakro. Kāla-cakro means that going round in orbit, that is also limited. So many millions of years you can go on like that. Just like if you take a small ball and you throw in the sky, it also rounds and again falls down. Similarly, all these planets they are going round the orbit by the order of the Supreme. That is called Saṅkarṣaṇa. So, all this, this is also mystic power. Such a huge lump of matter, the sun, which is fourteen hundred thousand times bigger than this earth, it is also floating in the sky. This is called yogeśvara. This is called mystic power. Not that I make something like this, I become God. This is one of the mystic power. There are so many other mystic powers.

So one who possesses all this mystic power, inconceivable by us, He is God. That mystic power is possessed by Kṛṣṇa. Therefore it is specifically mentioned, brūhi yogeśvare kṛṣṇe. Not anyone else. Because cent-percent mystic power is possessed by Kṛṣṇa. Others may possess ninety-nine, ninety-six, ninety or fifty-five or eighty, go on, go on, go on, go on. So in this way a living entity is part and parcel of Kṛṣṇa; he also can get mystic power up to seventy-eight percent. That is also not fully. Minutely.

When a living entity is free from material contamination, he can acquire the mystic power of Kṛṣṇa up to seventy-eight percent in minute quantity. Lord Brahmā, he is also a jīva, a living entity, but he has perfectly this seventy-eight percent mystic power in minute quantity, Brahmā. Lord Śiva has got perfectly eighty-five percent. Nārāyaṇa has got ninety-six percent. These are analyzed; these are not fictitious. But Kṛṣṇa has got full, cent-percent mystic powers. That is Kṛṣṇa. Therefore it is specifically mentioned, brūhi yogeśvare kṛṣṇe brahmaṇye dharma.

S.B.1.1.23

Wonderful mystic demonstrations

anye ca māyino māyām

antardhānādbhutātmanām

mayaṁ prakalpya vatsaṁ te

duduhur dhāraṇāmayīm

Translation

Others also, the inhabitants of planets known as Kimpuruṣa-loka, made the demon Maya into a calf, and they milked out mystic powers by which one can disappear immediately from another's vision and appear again in a different form.

Purport

It is said that the inhabitants of Kimpuruṣa-loka can perform many wonderful mystic demonstrations. In other words, they can exhibit as many wonderful things as one can imagine. The inhabitants of this planet can do whatever they like, or whatever they imagine. Such powers are also mystic powers. The possession of such mystic power is called īśitā. The demons generally learn such mystic powers by the practice of yoga. In the Daśama-skandha (Tenth Canto) of Śrīmad-Bhāgavatam, there is a vivid description of how the demons appear before Kṛṣṇa in various wonderful forms. For instance, Bakāsura appeared before Kṛṣṇa and His cowherd boyfriends as a gigantic crane. While present on this planet, Lord Kṛṣṇa had to fight with many demons who could exhibit the wonderful mystic powers of Kimpuruṣa-loka. Although the inhabitants of Kimpuruṣa-loka are naturally endowed with such powers, one can attain these powers on this planet by performing different yogic practices.

ŚB 4.18.20

CHAPTER TWO

MYSTIC PERFECTIONS

The Mystic Perfections achieved by actually successful yogis are 8 in number anima siddhi refers to the power by which one can become so small that he can enter into a stone modern scientific experiments enable us to enter into stone because they provide for Excavating so many Subways penetrating the hills Etc so anima siddhi the Mystic Perfection of trying to enter into stone has also been achieved by Material Science similarly all of the yoga siddhis or Perfections or material arts for example in the One Yoga Siddhi there is development of the power to become so light that one can float in the air or on water that is also being performed by modern scientists so they are flying in the air they are floating on the surface of the water and they are traveling under the water after comparing all these Mystic yoga siddhis to materialistic Perfections we find that the materialistic scientists try for the same Perfections so actually there is no difference between Mystic Perfection and materialistic Perfection a German scholar once said that the so-called yoga Perfections had already been achieved by these modern scientist and so he was not concerned with them.

1.00

He Intelligently went to India to learn how he could understand his eternal relationship with the Supreme Lord by means of bhakti yoga devotional service So the impersonalists have the Perfections that is Eightfold Perfections even the devotees will have these Eightfold perfections devotees of lord Krishna they are not devoid of anything as In the Tantra Sastra Lord Shiva is telling here to his wife Sati those devotees who are surrendered unto Lord Krishna those who have developed pure love towards Lord Krishna they are awarded all kinds of Perfections which the impersonalist also desire.

2.00

So normally the impersonalists have the Eightfold Perfections anima, laghima, isita, vasita, prakamya somany Perfections are there hypnotizing someone creating a planet destroying a planet becoming smaller than the smallest bigger than the biggest like that so many Perfections are there one can become light one can become heavy one can float in the air so many Perfections are there anima means one can become smaller very minute one can become very small and also there are many other Perfections one can float on the water, fly in the sky.

3.00

Entering into a stone nowadays modern scientists also discovered so many machines they are flying in the sky through the aeroplane, helicopter and they are also using drone they are floating on the surface of the water through the ships cruise ships and they are traveling under the water during Warfare by submarines they are traveling on the surface of the water and they are traveling under the water they are flying in the air they are drilling/ Excavating the earth or making Subways they are penetrating the Hills

4.00

So in this way so many things are being done by the moderns materialistic scientists whereas the Mystic Perfections yoga siddhi is also similar to that one can become smaller than smaller one can become bigger than the biggest one can float in the sky and one can float in the water one can float under the water or enter a stone and create a planet destroy a planet one can become smaller very heavy one can become very light so many Perfections are there all these things are being achieved by the modern materialistic scientists there is a story here there is one German scholar he knowing about the yoga Perfections he said it is already achieved by the modern scientists so he was not concerned with the perfections/ achievements of Ashtanga Yoga so he was interested in learning about the bhakti yoga devotional service so he came to India to learn about bhakti yoga.

5.00 about devotional service so there are many Perfections which the modern materialist scientists have not achieved yet it is said that they are sending satellites to Moon,Mars planets like that always researching they placed so many satellites in the antariksha outer space so many things are happening they have achieved so many Perfections but however certain Perfections are not yet achieved by the modern materialistic scientists.

6.00 A Yogi can enter into sun Planet just by using the rays of the sunshine this Perfections is called laghima similarly a Yogi can touch the

Moon with his finger though the modern astronauts go to the Moon with help of spaceships they undergo many difficulties whereas person with prapti siddhi perfection can extend his hand to touch the Moon with his finger so there are various Perfections which the modern scientists have not achieved whereas path of yoga Ashtanga Yoga processes one will achieve those Perfections if one performs astanga yoga one will undoubtedly achieve the various Perfections. nowadays we utilize various machines to do various activities but without using any machines just by the mano Vega by mind just by the will power one can achieve many things if He desires something he will achieve that is a different kind of perfection

7.00

those days the yogis had various kinds of Perfections but right now everything is mechanized machine learning artificial intelligence, computers, Android phones, mobiles, satellites, TV, theatres so many things we are utilizing whereas those days just by the will without the use of any machine they can achieve many things nowadays we are utilizing so many machines for calculation there is a calculator machine for typing there is a typing machine or for reading computer Machine nowadays artificial intelligence, Robots has come these are all some kind of atheistic inventions

8.00 those days there was no need of so many machines they had everything just by the desire just by the will they get everything and there is another Perfection siddhi which is called prapti siddhi or acquisition with this prapthi siddhi not only can the perfect Mystic yogi touch sun Planet but he can extend his hand anywhere and take whatever he likes he may be sitting thousands of miles away from certain place and if he likes he can take fruit from a garden There this is called prapti siddhi if one desires to take something from somewhere he can take it immediately that is a prapti siddhi acquisition right now we are seeing over the internet if you want to see some sports we are seeing through the Live program some aarti Temple in a temple the place may be very far away just like mayapur vrindavan two thousand three thousand kilometers maybe someone from America they can see what is happening in mayapur so that is also great Perfection through satellites they are watching what is happening in India mayapur

9.00

by sitting in front of a mobile or in front of a TV in front of a computer they could able to watch what's happening in faraway places that is another Perfection/achievement the modern scientist manufactured nuclear weapons with which they can destroy an insignificant part of this planet but by the yoga siddhi known as Ishita one can create and destroy an entire planet simply At will so this is another Perfection out of the Asta siddhis there is another Perfection called Ishita – it means

10.00 right now we are utilizing various weapons, various nuclear bombs are created various things are created because of these nuclear weapons a part of the Earth planet is destroyed during the Second World War Hiroshima, Nagasaki was destroyed by the American nuclear bombs whereas a Yogi can destroy entire planet if desires to destroy right now the scientists have the Perfection of destroying a place in a Earth planet like Hiroshima Nagasaki one or two lakhs of people were destroyed same kind of nuclear bombs

11.00

Were there in those days also ashwathama has sent brahmastra to destroy parikshit Maharaja in the womb of uttara ashwatama has also sent brahmastra to destroy Arjuna when he was in a dangerous position so like that there is a brahmastra two times Lord Krishna has saved the world 1st when the brahmastra was sent to destroy Arjuna Lord Krishna gave the direction to counteract the brahamastra with another brahmastra another time brahmastra was being sent to destroy the embryo of uttara parikshit Maharaj Lord Krishna has personally saved the pariskhit Maharaja so like that there is always some kind of weapons are being invented by the evil forces the Demonic Kings or Demonic rulers of the modern kaliyuga they are creating various things in the name of Defense they are creating various devastating situations they are creating various dangerous situation.

12.15

By this perfection one can bring anyone under his control this is a kind of hypnotism which is almost irresistible so nowadays we are applying various Tilaka, Gopichandana, Sindhur on Our Forehead which has been applied to protect ourselves from the evil forces from hypnotism black magic so this is a kind of hypnotism nowadays people do not apply Gopichandana, Tilaka, Sindhur because of which they are hypnotized by the various evil forces it's almost irresistible.

13.00

Sometimes it is found that the yogi who may have attained a little perfection in vasita Mystic power comes out among the people and speaks all sorts of nonsense controls their minds exploits them takes their money and then goes away just like putana came and she has hypnotized the gopalakas gopis elderly gopalakas and gopis she has hypnotized even yashoda and she has taken balakrishna baby Krishna and in that way agasura he has also hypnotized the gopala friends of lord Krishna and he has swallowed many gopala friends as well as the calves of the gopalakas so like that there is hypnotism attracting somebody and diverting their attention.

CHAPTER THREE

HOW TO ACHIEVE MYSTIC PERFECTION

ŚB 11.15.2

Śrī Uddhava said: My dear Lord Acyuta, by what process can mystic perfection be achieved, and what is the nature of such perfection? How many mystic perfections are there? Please explain these things to me. Indeed, You are the bestower of all mystic perfections.

ŚB 11.15.3

śrī-bhagavān uvāca
siddhayo 'ṣṭādaśa proktā
dhāraṇā yoga-pāra-gaiḥ
tāsām aṣṭau mat-pradhānā
daśaiva guṇa-hetavaḥ

Translation

The Supreme Personality of Godhead said: The masters of the yoga system have declared that there are eighteen types of mystic perfection and meditation, of which eight are primary, having their shelter in Me, and ten are secondary, appearing from the material mode of goodness.

Purport

Śrīla Viśvanātha Cakravartī Ṭhākura explains the word mat pradhānāḥ as follows. Lord Kṛṣṇa is naturally the shelter of the eight primary mystic potencies and meditations because such perfections emanate from the Lord's personal potency, and thus they are fully developed only within the Lord Himself and the Lord's personal associates. When materialistic persons mechanically acquire such potencies, the perfections awarded are of an inferior degree and are considered to be manifestations of māyā, illusion. A pure devotee of the Lord automatically receives from the Lord wonderful potencies to execute his devotional service. If for sense gratification one mechanically endeavors to acquire mystic perfections, then these perfections are certainly considered to be inferior expansions of the Lord's external potency.

ŚB 11.15.4-5

aṇimā mahimā mūrter
laghimā prāptir indriyaiḥ
prākāmyaṁ śruta-dṛṣṭeṣu
śakti-preraṇam īśitā

guṇeṣv asaṅgo vaśitā
yat-kāmas tad avasyati
etā me siddhayaḥ saumya
aṣṭāv autpattikā matāḥ

Translation

Among the eight primary mystic perfections, the three by which one transforms one's own body are aṇimā, becoming smaller than the smallest; mahimā, becoming greater than the greatest; and laghimā, becoming lighter than the lightest. Through the perfection of prāpti one acquires whatever one desires, and through prākāmya-siddhi one experiences any enjoyable object, either in this world or the next. Through īśitā-siddhi one can manipulate the subpotencies of māyā, and through the controlling potency called vaśitā-siddhi one is unimpeded by the three modes of nature. One who has acquired kāmāvasāyitā-siddhi can obtain anything from anywhere, to the highest possible limit. My dear gentle Uddhava, these eight mystic perfections are considered to be naturally existing and unexcelled within this world.

Purport

Through aṇimā-siddhi one can become so small that one can enter a stone or pass through any obstacle. Through mahimā-siddhi one becomes so great that one covers everything, and through laghimā one becomes so light that one can ride on the sun's rays into the sun planet. Through prāpti-siddhi one can acquire anything from anywhere and can even touch the moon with one's finger. By this mystic perfection one can also enter into the senses of any other living entity through the predominating deities of the particular senses; and by thus utilizing the senses of others, one can acquire anything. Through prākāmya one can experience any enjoyable object, either in this world or the next, and through īśitā, or the controlling potency, one can manipulate the subpotencies of māyā, which are material. In other words, even by acquiring mystic powers one cannot pass beyond the control of illusion; however, one may manipulate the subpotencies of illusion. Through vaśitā, or the power to control, one can bring others under one's dominion or keep oneself beyond the control of the three modes of nature. Ultimately, one acquires through kāmāvasāyitā the maximum powers of control, acquisition and enjoyment. The word autpattikāḥ in this verse indicates being original, natural and unexcelled. These eight mystic potencies originally exist in the Supreme Personality of Godhead, Kṛṣṇa, in the superlative degree. Lord Kṛṣṇa becomes so small that He enters within the atomic particles, and He becomes so large that as Mahā-Viṣṇu He breathes out millions of universes. The Lord can become so light or subtle that even great mystic yogīs cannot perceive Him, and the Lord's acquisitive power is perfect, because He keeps the total existence eternally within His body. The Lord certainly can enjoy whatever He likes, control all energies, dominate all other persons and exhibit complete omnipotency. Therefore it is to be understood that these eight mystic perfections are insignificant expansions of the mystic potency of the Lord, who in Bhagavad-gītā is called Yogeśvara, the Supreme Lord of all mystic potencies. These eight perfections are not artificial, but are natural and unexcelled because they originally exist in the Supreme Personality of Godhead.

ŚB 11.15.6-7

anūrmimattvaṁ dehe 'smin
dūra-śravaṇa-darśanam
mano-javaḥ kāma-rūpaṁ
para-kāya-praveśanam

svacchanda-mṛtyur devānāṁ
saha-krīḍānudarśanam
yathā-saṅkalpa-saṁsiddhir
ājñāpratihatā gatiḥ

Translation

The ten secondary mystic perfections arising from the modes of nature are the powers of freeing oneself from hunger and thirst and other bodily disturbances, hearing and seeing things far away, moving the body at the speed of the mind, assuming any form one desires, entering the bodies of others, dying when one desires, witnessing the pastimes between the demigods and the celestial girls called Apsarās, completely executing one's determination and giving orders whose fulfillment is unimpeded.

ŚB 11.15.8-9

tri-kāla-jñatvam advandvaṁ
para-cittādy-abhijñatā
agny-arkāmbu-viṣādīnāṁ
pratiṣṭambho 'parājayaḥ

etāś coddeśataḥ proktā
yoga-dhāraṇa-siddhayaḥ
yayā dhāraṇayā yā syād
yathā vā syān nibodha me

Translation

The power to know past, present and future; tolerance of heat, cold and other dualities; knowing the minds of others; checking the influence of fire, sun, water, poison, and so on; and remaining unconquered by others — these constitute five perfections of the mystic process of yoga and meditation. I am simply listing these here according to their names and characteristics. Now please learn from Me how specific mystic perfections arise from specific meditations and also of the particular processes involved.

Purport

According to the ācāryas these five perfections are considered to be quite inferior to the others already mentioned, since they involve more or less ordinary physical and mental manipulations. According to Śrīla Madhvācārya, in the perfection called agny-arkāmbu-viṣādīnāṁ pratiṣṭambhaḥ, or checking the influence of fire, sun, water, poison, and so on, the term "and so on" refers to one's remaining invulnerable to all types of weapons as well as attacks by nails, teeth, beating, curses and other such sources.

ŚB 11.15.10

bhūta-sūkṣmātmani mayi
tan-mātraṁ dhārayen manaḥ
aṇimānam avāpnoti
tan-mātropāsako mama

Translation

One who worships Me in My atomic form pervading all subtle elements, fixing his mind on that alone, obtains the mystic perfection called aṇimā.

Purport

Aṇimā refers to the mystic ability to make oneself smaller than the smallest and thus able to enter within anything. The Supreme Personality of Godhead is within the atoms and atomic particles, and one who perfectly fixes his mind in that subtle atomic form of the Lord acquires the mystic potency called aṇimā, by which one can enter within even the most dense matter such as stone.

ŚB 11.15.11

mahat-tattvātmani mayi

yathā-saṁsthaṁ mano dadhat

mahimānam avāpnoti

bhūtānāṁ ca pṛthak pṛthak

Translation

One who absorbs his mind in the particular form of the mahat-tattva and thus meditates upon Me as the Supreme Soul of the total material existence achieves the mystic perfection called mahimā. By further absorbing the mind in the situation of each individual element such as the sky, air, fire, and so on, one progressively acquires the greatness of each material element.

Purport

There are innumerable verses in Vedic literatures explaining that the Supreme Personality of Godhead is qualitatively not different from His creation and thus a yogī may meditate upon the total material existence as a manifestation of the external potency of the Lord. Once the yogī has established his realization that the material creation is not different from the Lord, he obtains the perfection called mahimā-siddhi. By realizing the Lord's presence in each individual element the yogī also acquires the greatness of each element. However, the pure devotees are not very interested in such perfections because they are surrendered to the Personality of Godhead, who exhibits such perfections to the infinite degree. Being always protected by the Lord, the pure devotees save their precious time to chant Hare Kṛṣṇa, Hare Kṛṣṇa, Kṛṣṇa Kṛṣṇa, Hare Hare/ Hare Rāma, Hare Rāma, Rāma Rāma, Hare Hare. Thus they achieve for themselves and others saṁsiddhi, or the supreme perfection, pure love of Godhead, Kṛṣṇa consciousness, by which one expands one's existence beyond the total material creation to the spiritual planets called Vaikuṇṭha.

ŚB 11.15.12

paramāṇu-maye cittaṁ
bhūtānāṁ mayi rañjayan
kāla-sūkṣmārthatāṁ yogī
laghimānam avāpnuyāt

Translation

I exist within everything, and I am therefore the essence of the atomic constituents of material elements. By attaching his mind to Me in this form, the yogī may achieve the perfection called laghimā, by which he realizes the subtle atomic substance of time.

Purport

Śrīmad-Bhāgavatam elaborately explains that kāla, or time, is the transcendental form of the Lord that moves the material world. Since the five gross elements are composed of atoms, the atomic particles are the subtle substance or manifestation of the movements of time. More subtle than time is the Personality of Godhead Himself, who expands His potency as the time factor. By understanding all these things clearly the yogī obtains laghimā-siddhi, or the power to make himself lighter than the lightest.

ŚB 11.15.13

dhārayan mayy ahaṁ-tattve
mano vaikārike 'khilam
sarvendriyāṇām ātmatvaṁ
prāptiṁ prāpnoti man-manāḥ

Translation

Fixing his mind completely in Me within the element of false ego generated from the mode of goodness, the yogī obtains the power of mystic acquisition, by which he becomes the proprietor of the senses of all living entities. He obtains such perfection because his mind is absorbed in Me.

Purport

It is significant that in order to acquire each mystic perfection one must fix one's mind on the Supreme Personality of Godhead. Śrīla Bhaktisiddhānta Sarasvatī Ṭhākura states that those who pursue such perfections without fixing the mind in the Supreme Lord acquire a gross and inferior reflection of each mystic potency. Those who are not conscious of the Lord cannot actually synchronize their minds perfectly with the universal functions and therefore cannot elevate their mystic opulences to the universal platform.

ŚB 11.15.14

mahaty ātmani yaḥ sūtre
dhārayen mayi mānasam
prakāmyaṁ pārameṣṭhyaṁ me
vindate 'vyakta-janmanaḥ

Translation

One who concentrates all mental activities in Me as the Supersoul of that phase of the mahat-tattva which manifests the chain of fruitive activities obtains from Me, whose appearance is beyond material perception, the most excellent mystic perfection called prakāmya.

Purport

Śrīla Vīrarāghava Ācārya explains that the word sūtra, or "thread," is used to indicate that the mahat-tattva sustains one's fruitive activities just as a thread sustains a row of jewels. Thus by fixed meditation on the Supreme Personality of Godhead, who is the soul of the mahat-tattva, one can achieve the most excellent perfection called prakāmya. Avyakta-janmanaḥ indicates that the Supreme Personality of Godhead appears from the avyakta, or the spiritual sky, or that His birth is avyakta, beyond the perception of material senses. Unless one accepts the transcendental form of the Supreme Personality of Godhead, there is no possibility of obtaining prakāmya or any other genuine mystic perfection.

ŚB 11.15.15

viṣṇau try-adhīśvare cittaṁ
dhārayet kāla-vigrahe
sa īśitvam avāpnoti
kṣetrajña-kṣetra-codanām

Translation

One who places his consciousness on Viṣṇu, the Supersoul, the prime mover and Supreme Lord of the external energy consisting of three modes, obtains the mystic perfection of controlling other conditioned souls, their material bodies and their bodily designations.

Purport

We should remember that mystic perfection never enables a living entity to challenge the supremacy of the Personality of Godhead. In fact, one cannot obtain such perfections without the mercy of the Supreme Lord; thus one's controlling power can never disturb the plan of Lord Kṛṣṇa. One is allowed to exhibit mystic control only within the confines of the law of God, and even a great yogī who transgresses the law of God by his so-called mystic opulences will be severely punished, as revealed in the story of Durvāsā Muni cursing Ambarīṣa Mahārāja.

CHAPTER FOUR

Divine and Demoniac Mystic Powers

Pradyumna Born to Kṛṣṇa and Rukmiṇī, CHAPTER 55 Krishna Book

It is said that Cupid, who is directly part and parcel of Lord Vāsudeva and who was formerly burned to ashes by the anger of Lord Śiva, took birth from the womb of Rukmiṇī, begotten by Kṛṣṇa. This is Kāmadeva, a demigod of the heavenly planets especially capable of inducing lusty desires. The Supreme Personality of Godhead, Kṛṣṇa, has many grades of parts and parcels, but the quadruple expansions of Kṛṣṇa – Vāsudeva, Saṅkarṣaṇa, Pradyumna and Aniruddha – are directly in the Viṣṇu category. Kāma, or the Cupid demigod, who later took his birth from the womb of Rukmiṇī, was also named Pradyumna, but he cannot be the Pradyumna of the Viṣṇu category. He belongs to the category of jīva-tattva, but for exhibiting special power in the category of demigods he was a part and parcel of the superprowess of Pradyumna. That is the verdict of the Gosvāmīs. Therefore, when Cupid was burned to ashes by the anger of Lord Śiva, he merged into the body of Vāsudeva, and to get his body again he was begotten in the womb of Rukmiṇī by Lord Kṛṣṇa Himself. Thus he was born as the son of Kṛṣṇa and celebrated by the name Pradyumna. Because he was begotten by Lord Kṛṣṇa directly, his qualities were most similar to those of Kṛṣṇa.

There was a demon of the name Śambara who was destined to be killed by Pradyumna. The Śambara demon knew of his destiny, and as soon as he learned that Pradyumna had been born, he took the shape of a woman and kidnapped the baby from the maternity home less than ten days after his birth. The demon took him and threw him directly into the sea. But, as it is said, "Whoever is protected by Kṛṣṇa, no one can kill, and whoever is destined to be killed by Kṛṣṇa, no one can protect." When Pradyumna was thrown into the sea, a big fish immediately swallowed him. Later this fish was caught in the net of a fisherman, and the fish was later sold to the Śambara demon. In the kitchen of the demon was a maidservant whose name was Māyāvatī. This woman had formerly been the wife of Cupid, called Rati. When the fish was presented to the demon Śambara, it was taken charge of by his cook, who was to make it into a palatable fish preparation. Demons and Rākṣasas are accustomed to eating meat, fish and similar nonvegetarian foods. Demons like Rāvaṇa, Kaṁsa and Hiraṇyakaśipu, although born of brāhmaṇa and kṣatriya fathers, used to take meat and fish without discrimination. This practice is still prevalent in India, and those who eat meat and fish are generally called demons and Rākṣasas.

When the cook was cutting the fish, he found within its stomach a nice baby, which he immediately presented to the charge of Māyāvatī, who was an assistant in the kitchen affairs. This woman was surprised to see how such a nice baby could remain within the belly of a fish, and the situation perplexed her. The great sage Nārada then appeared and explained to her about the birth of Pradyumna and how the baby had been taken away by Śambara and later thrown into the sea. In this way the whole story was disclosed to Māyāvatī. Māyāvatī knew that she had previously been Rati, the wife of Cupid; after her husband was burned to ashes by the wrath of Lord Śiva, she was always expecting him to come back in a material form. This woman was engaged for cooking rice and dāl in the kitchen, but when she got this nice baby and understood that he was Cupid, her own husband, she naturally took charge of him and with great affection began to bathe him regularly. Miraculously, the baby swiftly grew up, and within a very short period he became a beautiful young man. His eyes were just like the petals of lotus flowers, and his arms were long, reaching down to his knees; any woman who happened to see him was captivated by his bodily beauty.

Māyāvatī could understand that her former husband, Cupid, born as Pradyumna, had grown into such a nice young man, and she also gradually became captivated and lusty. Smiling before him with a feminine attractiveness, she expressed her desire for sexual union. He therefore inquired from her, "How is it possible that first you were affectionate like a mother and now you are expressing the symptoms of a lusty woman? What is the reason for such a change?" On hearing this statement from Pradyumna, the woman, Rati, replied, "My dear sir, you are the son of Lord Kṛṣṇa. Before you were ten days old, you were stolen by the Śambara demon and later thrown into the water and swallowed by a fish. In this way you have come under my care, but actually, in your former life as Cupid, I was your wife; therefore, my manifestation of conjugal symptoms is not at all incompatible. Śambara wanted to kill you, and he is endowed with various mystic powers. Therefore, before he again attempts to kill you, please kill him as soon as possible with your divine power. Since you were stolen by Śambara, your mother, Rukmiṇī-devī, has been in a very grievous condition, like a kurarī bird who has lost her babies. She is very affectionate toward you, and since you have been taken away from her, she has been living like a cow aggrieved over the loss of its calf."

Māyāvatī had mystic knowledge of supernatural powers. Supernatural powers are generally known as māyā, and to surpass all such powers there is another supernatural power, called mahā-māyā. Māyāvatī had the knowledge of the mystic power of mahā-māyā, and she delivered to Pradyumna this specific energetic power in order to defeat the mystic powers of the Śambara demon. Thus being empowered by his wife, Pradyumna immediately went before Śambara and challenged him to fight. Pradyumna addressed him in very strong language, so that his temper would be agitated and he would be moved to fight. At Pradyumna's words, the demon Śambara, being insulted, felt just as a snake feels after being struck by someone's foot. A serpent cannot tolerate being kicked by another animal or by a man, and it immediately bites its opponent.

Śambara felt the words of Pradyumna as if they were a kick. He immediately took his club in his hand and appeared before Pradyumna to fight. Roaring like a thundering cloud, in great anger the demon began to beat Pradyumna with his club, just as a thunderbolt beats a mountain. Pradyumna protected himself with his own club and eventually struck the demon very severely. In this way, the fighting between Śambarāsura and Pradyumna began in earnest.

But Śambarāsura knew the art of mystic powers and could raise himself into the sky and fight from outer space. There is a demon of the name Maya, and Śambarāsura had learned many mystic powers from him. He thus raised himself high into the sky and threw various types of nuclear weapons at the body of Pradyumna. To combat the mystic powers of Śambarāsura, Pradyumna invoked another mystic power, known as mahāvidyā, which was different from the black mystic power. The mahāvidyā mystic power is based on the quality of goodness. Śambara, understanding that his enemy was formidable, took assistance from various kinds of demoniac mystic powers belonging to the Guhyakas, the Gandharvas, the Piśācas, the snakes and the Rākṣasas. But although the demon exhibited his mystic powers and took shelter of supernatural strength, Pradyumna was able to counteract his strength and powers by the superior power of mahāvidyā. When Śambarāsura was defeated in every respect, Pradyumna took his sharp sword and immediately cut off the demon's head, which was decorated with a helmet and valuable jewels. When Pradyumna thus killed the demon, all the demigods in the higher planetary systems showered flowers on him.

Pradyumna's wife, Māyāvatī, could travel in outer space, and therefore they directly reached Dvārakā, his father's capital, by the airways. They passed above the palace of Lord Kṛṣṇa and came down as a cloud comes down with lightning. The inner section of a palace is known as the antaḥ-pura (private apartments). Pradyumna and Māyāvatī could see many women there, and they set down among them. When the women saw Pradyumna, dressed in yellowish garments, with very long arms, curling hair, beautiful reddish eyes, a smiling face, jewelry and ornaments, they at first could not recognize him as a personality different from Kṛṣṇa. They all felt very bashful at the sudden presence of Kṛṣṇa and wanted to hide in a different corner of the palace.

When the women saw, however, that not all the characteristics of Lord Kṛṣṇa were present in the personality of Pradyumna, out of curiosity they came back to see him and his wife, Māyāvatī. All of them were conjecturing as to who he was, for he was so beautiful. Among the women was Rukmiṇī-devī, who was equally beautiful, with her lotuslike eyes. Seeing Pradyumna, she naturally remembered her own son, and milk began to flow from her breasts out of motherly affection. She then began to wonder, "Who is this beautiful young boy? He appears to be the most beautiful person. Who is the fortunate young woman able to conceive this nice boy in her womb and become his mother? And who is that young woman who has accompanied him? How have they met? Remembering my own son, who was stolen from the maternity home, I can only guess that if he is living somewhere, he might have grown by this time to be like this boy." Simply by intuition, Rukmiṇī could understand that Pradyumna was her own lost son. She could also observe that Pradyumna resembled Lord Kṛṣṇa in every respect. She was struck with wonder as to how he had acquired all the characteristics of Lord Kṛṣṇa. She therefore began to think more confidently that the boy must be her own grown-up son because she felt so much affection for him, and, as an auspicious sign, her left arm was trembling.

At that very moment, Lord Kṛṣṇa, along with His father and mother, Devakī and Vasudeva, appeared on the scene. Kṛṣṇa, the Supreme Personality of Godhead, could understand everything, yet in that situation He remained silent. However, by the desire of Lord Śrī Kṛṣṇa, the great sage Nārada also appeared, and he disclosed all the incidents – how Pradyumna had been stolen from the maternity home and how he had grown up and had come there with his wife, Māyāvatī, who had formerly been Rati, the wife of Cupid. When everyone was informed of the mysterious disappearance of Pradyumna and how he had grown up, they were all struck with wonder because they had gotten back their dead son after they were almost hopeless of his return. When they understood that it was Pradyumna who was present, they received him with great delight. One after another, all the members of the family – Devakī, Vasudeva, Lord Śrī Kṛṣṇa, Lord Balarāma, Rukmiṇī and all the women of the family – embraced Pradyumna and his wife, Māyāvatī. When the news of Pradyumna's return spread all over the city of Dvārakā, all the astonished citizens came with great eagerness to see the lost Pradyumna. "The dead son has come back," they said. "What can be more pleasing than this?"

Śrīla Śukadeva Gosvāmī has explained that in the beginning all the ladies of the palace, who were all mothers and stepmothers of Pradyumna, mistook him to be Kṛṣṇa and were all bashful, infected by the desire for conjugal love. The explanation is that Pradyumna's personal appearance was exactly like Kṛṣṇa's, and he was factually Cupid himself. There was no cause for astonishment, therefore, when the mothers of Pradyumna and the other women mistook him in that way. It is clear from this statement that Pradyumna's bodily characteristics were so similar to Kṛṣṇa's that he was mistaken for Kṛṣṇa even by his mother.